MW01618191

For Liam, 'uh' you.

Family Style by Sally Shum McDevitt
Published by Sally Shum McDevitt

Copyright © 2022 Sally Shum McDevitt
All rights reserved. No portion of this book may be reproduced in any form without permission from the publisher, except as permitted by U.S. copyright law. For permissions contact: sallysmcdevitt@gmail.com

ISBN: 978-0-578-34492-8 (print)
Printed in USA
First Edition

FAMILY STYLE

My family loves to

EAT!

We gather around,

we take a seat.

Dishes

appear

upon

the table.

We eat
as much
as we are
able.

I get to choose
from all the cuisine,

(so long as there
is something green).

Some Sundays we go to get

Dim Sum.

The tiny dishes are

yum, yum, yum!

While we're there,
we love to talk.

Wei, leng loi!

But afterwards,
we have to walk.

On winter nights we make

hot pot.

(We'll make it any chance
we've got).

We sluurrrp

our noodles

and

dunk

our meat.

You can't stay cold

with all that heat!

No matter the dish,
I'll always smile.

Sik fan!

When I get to eat food

Made in the USA
Monee, IL
20 December 2021